BASEBALL
RECORD BREAKERS

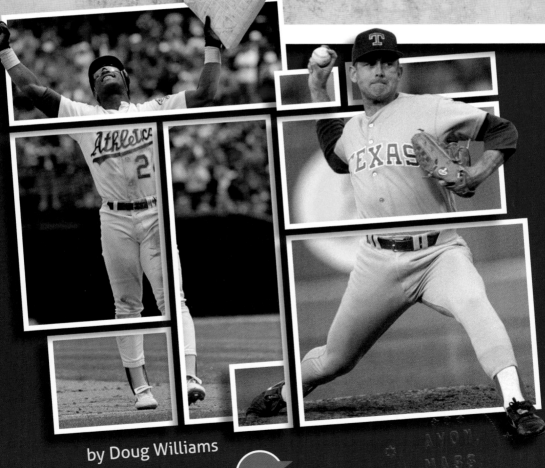

by Doug Williams

SportsZone
An Imprint of Abdo Publishing | abdopublishing.com

abdopublishing.com

Published by Abdo Publishing, a division of ABDO, PO Box 398166,
Minneapolis, Minnesota 55439. Copyright © 2016 by Abdo Consulting
Group, Inc. International copyrights reserved in all countries. No part of this
book may be reproduced in any form without written permission from the
publisher. SportsZone™ is a trademark and logo of Abdo Publishing.

Printed in the United States of America, North Mankato, Minnesota
032015
092015

THIS BOOK CONTAINS
RECYCLED MATERIALS

Cover Photo: Eric Risberg/AP Images, cover (left); Nikitin/AP Images,
cover (right)
Interior Photos: Bob Wands/AP Images, 5; AP Images, 7, 11, 23, 25, 44, 45; The
Rucker Archive/Icon Sportswire, 8; Susan Ragan/AP Images, 13; Bill Janscha/
AP Images, 14; Pete Leabo/AP Images, 17; Gene Puskar/AP Images, 18; Eric
Risberg/AP Images, 20; Ray Stubblebine/AP Images, 26; Denis Paquin/AP
Images, 29; Wilfredo Lee/AP Images, 30; Lenny Ignelzi/AP Images, 32; National
Baseball Library/AP Images, 35; Daniel M. Silva/Shutterstock Images, 36; John
Dunn/AP Images, 38; Eric Gay/AP Images, 41; Matt Slocum/AP Images, 42

Editor: Patrick Donnelly
Series Designer: Nikki Farinella

Library of Congress Control Number: 2015931672

Cataloging-in-Publication Data
Williams, Doug.
 Baseball record breakers / Doug Williams.
  p. cm. -- (Record breakers)
Includes bibliographical references and index.
ISBN 978-1-62403-845-7
1. Baseball--Juvenile literature. 2. Baseball--Records--Juvenile literature.
I. Title.
796.357--dc23
                                                            2015931672

TABLE OF CONTENTS

Note: All records in this book are current through the 2014 MLB season.

1

JOLTIN' JOE'S STREAK

New York Yankees center fielder Joe DiMaggio was in a slump. As he walked up to home plate on the afternoon of May 15, 1941, he had not had a hit in two games. His batting average had dropped 67 points since May 1. He did not look like the same player who won the American League (AL) batting championship the past two years.

But in the bottom of the first inning at Yankee Stadium, DiMaggio got a fastball he liked from Chicago White Sox pitcher Eddie Smith. He hit a line drive to center field for a single.

Yankees star Joe DiMaggio made headlines in 1941 with the longest hitting streak in Major League Baseball (MLB) history.

At the time, DiMaggio's hit did not mean much. The Yankees would lose 13–1. Only 9,040 fans were there to see it. Yet the single was the start of something big. Through the rest of May, all of June, and well into July, "Joltin' Joe" got a hit in every game he played. His hitting streak lasted 56 games, a major league record.

The United States was on the brink of World War II. DiMaggio's streak was a nice distraction for many people. As his streak grew, news of his feats made its way onto the front pages of daily newspapers from New York to California.

DiMaggio paid little attention to it at first. He was just happy he was hitting again and the Yankees were winning. He said the key to getting hot was remembering to point his left foot toward the pitcher. It was something he'd learned in the minor leagues but had moved away from during his slump.

"Everybody asked what was wrong," DiMaggio said. "They told me I was striding too far. They told me I was upper-cutting the ball. They told me just about everything. And then on May 15 . . . I took a gander at my left foot. It wasn't pointed toward the pitcher at all. It was pointed toward first base."

Back in his familiar stance, DiMaggio started hitting the ball hard to all fields. On May 16 he had two hits—a home run and a triple. Two games later he had three hits. On May 27 he had four hits to run his streak to 12 games.

Joe DiMaggio rips a single to left field on June 29, 1941, to run his hitting streak to a record 42 straight games.

On June 7, DiMaggio had three hits in St. Louis against the Browns. The next day he had four hits, including three home runs, in a doubleheader. That extended his streak to 24 games.

"I knew I was hitting the ball well, but I wasn't conscious of the streak until after that series in St. Louis, when the

Ted Williams, *left*, and Joe DiMaggio both made history with remarkable hitting feats in 1941.

writers started digging out the records I could break," said DiMaggio.

On June 29 DiMaggio broke George Sisler's AL record of 41 straight games. On July 2 a home run against the Boston Red Sox pushed DiMaggio's streak to 45 games. That beat the previous major league record of 44 set by "Wee Willie" Keeler in 1897. That was before the AL even existed.

"I don't know how far I can go," he said at the time. "But I'm not going to worry about it now."

Between July 6 and July 16 he had two four-hit games and two three-hit games. As he prepared to play the Indians in Cleveland on July 17, DiMaggio had hit safely in 56 straight games.

Twice in his first three plate appearances that day, Indians third baseman Ken Keltner robbed him of hits. Then in his final at-bat, DiMaggio grounded into a double play. The streak was over.

"I can't say that I'm glad it's over," DiMaggio said. "Of course I wanted it to go on as long as it could."

DiMaggio hit .408 during the streak, raising his average to .375. The next day, he began a 16-game hitting streak. Pete Rose's 44-game streak in 1978 is the longest in the big leagues since 1941.

THE LAST .400 HITTER

ALSO IN 1941, TED WILLIAMS OF THE BOSTON RED SOX HIT .406. THOUGH SEVERAL PLAYERS HIT .400 OR BETTER BEFORE WILLIAMS, NO ONE HAS DONE IT SINCE. WILLIAMS ENTERED THE FINAL DAY OF THE SEASON BATTING .39955 AND THEN WENT 6-FOR-8 IN A DOUBLEHEADER TO REACH .406. HE HAD 185 HITS AND 147 WALKS IN 143 GAMES, GIVING HIM A SEASON-RECORD ON-BASE PERCENTAGE OF .553 THAT LASTED UNTIL 2002.

2 NOLAN'S
SEVEN NO-NOS

When a New York Mets scout first saw Nolan Ryan pitch, he could not believe his eyes. The tall, skinny, 17-year-old Texan was throwing unhittable fastballs.

"Has the best arm I've ever seen in my life," scout Red Murff wrote in his 1964 report to the Mets. "Could be a real power pitcher someday."

It turned out Murff had an eye for talent. Ryan became perhaps the most overpowering pitcher in history. He threw seven no-hitters, three more than any other pitcher. He also struck out a record 5,714 batters.

By 1966, Ryan was in the big leagues at age 19. In 1972 he led all of baseball in strikeouts. But in 1973 Ryan and his 100-mile-per-hour fastball truly became legends.

On May 15 of that season, Ryan threw his first no-hitter. He struck out 12 batters as his California Angels beat the Kansas City Royals 3–0.

On July 15 Ryan was even better. He struck out 17 without giving up a hit to beat the Detroit Tigers 6–0 in Detroit. No pitcher ever has had more strikeouts in a nine-inning no-hitter.

Tigers first baseman Norm Cash already had struck out twice when he came to bat with two outs in the bottom of the ninth. He was carrying a wooden leg from a table in the Detroit clubhouse instead of a bat.

When home plate umpire Ron Luciano noticed, he told Cash he could not use it. "Why not?" asked Cash. "I won't hit him anyway."

Ryan was overpowering that season. He struck out a record 383 batters while winning 21 games. At age 26 Ryan had proven that when his blazing fastball and big curveball were in control, hitters were in trouble.

"Every time he goes out there's a possibility of a no-no," said Angels general manager Harry Dalton. Oakland manager Dick Williams said many of his players often became ill on days they were scheduled to face Ryan. "They came down with a rare flu," he said. "I called it Nolanitis."

Nolan Ryan pitches for the Houston Astros in the 1986 NL Championship Series.

Most pitchers never throw one no-hitter, let alone two. But Ryan pitched five more:

September 28, 1974: He struck out 15 in a 4–0 victory over the Minnesota Twins.

June 1, 1975: His fourth and final no-hitter for the Angels was a 1–0 win over the Baltimore Orioles. He struck out nine. He tied Sandy Koufax for the most no-hitters thrown.

Nolan Ryan is carried off the field by his Texas Rangers teammates on May 1, 1991, after he threw his seventh career no-hitter.

September 26, 1981: Pitching for the Houston Astros, Ryan struck out 14 in a 5–0 win over the Los Angeles Dodgers. Ryan was now the no-hitter king.

June 11, 1990: Pitching for the Texas Rangers at age 43, Ryan struck out 14 in a 5–0 victory over the Oakland Athletics.

May 1, 1991: He struck out 16 in a 5–0 win over the Toronto Blue Jays.

Before his seventh no-hitter, there were no indications Ryan would even get through the first inning. At age 44, his back and ankle hurt. He told his pitching coach, "I feel old today."

Yet Ryan struck out the first batter and then settled into a groove. His fastball reached 96 mph. In the final inning, the Rangers crowd was chanting, "No-lan! No-lan!" Ryan struck out future Hall of Famer Roberto Alomar on a fastball to close out the game.

Along with seven no-hitters, Ryan also threw 12 one-hit games. His plaque at the Baseball Hall of Fame says it best: "One of baseball's most intimidating figures on the pitching mound for four decades."

BACK-TO-BACK MAGIC

JOHNNY VANDER MEER HAD A 13-YEAR PITCHING CAREER, BUT HE WAS NOT A STAR. HIS OVERALL RECORD WAS 119 WINS AND 121 LOSSES. BUT THE CINCINNATI REDS PITCHER THREW BACK-TO-BACK NO-HITTERS IN JUNE 1938. NO OTHER PITCHER HAS MATCHED HIM. SAID VANDER MEER, "SOMEBODY MIGHT TIE IT, BUT I DON'T THINK IT WILL EVER BE BROKEN."

3
RUNNING
RICKEY

Rickey Henderson had just drawn a walk. As he took his lead from first base, everyone in Milwaukee County Stadium knew Henderson would try to steal second.

The Oakland Athletics star had entered the game with 118 steals. That tied Lou Brock's 1974 record for most stolen bases in a season. Now, on the night of August 27, 1982, Henderson was eager to break Brock's record. Brock was even on hand to watch it happen.

Brewers pitcher Doc Medich threw over to first base to keep Henderson from getting a good lead. Then he threw over a second time. Then a third and fourth time.

Rickey Henderson tips his cap to the crowd in Milwaukee, Wisconsin, after he broke Lou Brock's MLB single-season record of 118 stolen bases on August 27, 1982.

Finally Medich threw to the plate. The Brewers had called a pitchout. The ball arrived high and outside. Catcher Ted Simmons came out of his crouch, caught the ball, and fired to second base.

Simmons made a perfect throw, right on the bag. But Henderson beat the tag. It was steal number 119.

Henderson pulled up the base and held it aloft. The crowd of 41,600 in Milwaukee gave him a standing ovation. The game was halted briefly while players and coaches congratulated Henderson.

After the game, Henderson said he was glad to get the record out of the way. "I'm relieved and exhausted," he said. But not so exhausted that he could not keep running.

Henderson stole three more bases in the game. He finished the season with 130 steals.

At age 23, Henderson was just getting started. He was in the fourth season of a 25-year career that would end with an induction into the Baseball Hall of Fame.

Henderson stole 108 bases in 1983 to lead the AL. It was his fourth straight stolen-base title. He went on to be the league's top base thief eight more times. Even at age 39 in 1998, he stole a league-best 66 bases.

But it was seven years earlier, on May 1, 1991, that Henderson became baseball's all-time steals leader. In the fourth inning of a game against the Yankees in Oakland,

Rickey Henderson was not just a great base-stealer—he was also one of the best leadoff hitters in MLB history.

Rickey Henderson slides headfirst into third base to set the record for most career stolen bases on May 1, 1991.

Henderson stole third base with a headfirst slide. That gave him 939 career stolen bases. Brock had held the record of 938 since his retirement in 1979.

Like the 1982 game against the Brewers, this game was also stopped for a brief ceremony. And again the ceremony featured Brock, who had become Henderson's friend. Brock told the crowd that Henderson was "maybe the greatest competitor who ever ran the bases." Said Henderson: "Lou Brock was a symbol of great base stealing, but today I am the greatest of all time."

The career stolen base record meant a great deal to Henderson. He had been driven to steal bases ever since high school. A guidance counselor had promised him a quarter for every base he stole. By the time he arrived in the big leagues at age 20, Henderson was already well known for his speed on the base paths.

Henderson was much more than a base stealer, however. When he retired after the 2003 season at age 44, he had 3,055 hits. His 2,295 runs scored and 1,406 stolen bases were each the most in major league history. He was a 10-time All-Star. He led off a game with a home run 81 times—another record. His combination of speed, power, and patience at the plate made him baseball's most dangerous leadoff hitter.

TY COBB, DUAL THREAT

LONG BEFORE LOU BROCK AND RICKEY HENDERSON WERE RUNNING THE BASES, TY COBB WAS BASEBALL'S MOST FEARED BASE STEALER. THE HALL OF FAME OUTFIELDER PLAYED FROM 1905 TO 1928. HE WAS FAST AND FEARLESS ON THE BASES. HE EVEN STOLE HOME 54 TIMES. AS A DETROIT TIGER IN 1915, HE STOLE 96 BASES, A RECORD THAT STOOD UNTIL 1962. HIS CAREER MARK OF 897 STEALS LASTED UNTIL 1977. COBB ALSO WON 12 BATTING CHAMPIONSHIPS AND HAD MORE THAN 4,000 HITS. HE HOLDS THE RECORD FOR HIGHEST CAREER BATTING AVERAGE AT .366.

4
THE
HIT KING

P ete Rose wasn't blessed with great strength, size, or speed. Standing just 5 feet 11 inches tall and weighing 192 pounds, he was stocky. He did not look like a gifted athlete.

But when Rose stepped into the batter's box and crouched low in his stance, he seemed to stare right through the pitcher. He looked like the most determined player on the field, because he was. The man who became known as "Charlie Hustle" made himself a great player through sheer force of will.

"I've never seen anyone as competitive as Pete," said longtime Cincinnati Reds teammate Tommy Helms.

Pete Rose used his unique batting style to slash out more hits than any player in MLB history.

Tony Perez, a Hall of Famer who came up with Rose in the Reds' minor league system, said Rose could not do much in his first season as a pro. "He wasn't that good a ballplayer," Perez said. "He wasn't a good hitter. He wasn't a fast runner. . . . He [worked] hard to be where he is."

On the night of September 11, 1985, Rose was at Riverfront Stadium in his hometown of Cincinnati. At age 44 in his twenty-third season, the Reds' player/manager had 4,191 career hits, tied with the great Ty Cobb for the most of all time. Rose admired Cobb, and he had been chasing his hit record a long time. Now, after three batting championships, 10 200-hit seasons, and seven times leading the National League (NL) in hits, Rose was one hit away from his goal. He almost could not believe it.

"Think about it," he said. "It will make me number one among all the people who ever played this game. And there've been a lot of people who've played."

On that night, Rose's Reds were playing the San Diego Padres. As Rose stepped to the plate against pitcher Eric Show in the bottom of the first inning, most of the 47,237 in attendance stood. Fans raised their cameras to capture history.

On Show's fourth pitch, Rose, batting left-handed, ripped a line drive to left field. It was a single for hit 4,192.

Pete Rose follows through on the swing that resulted in career hit 4,192 on September 11, 1985.

Pete Rose, *left*, earned the nickname "Charlie Hustle" for his breakneck style of play.

Immediately, fireworks exploded above the ballpark. Teammates rushed to mob him. A pair of Reds picked him up and carried him on their shoulders.

The ovation for Rose lasted nearly seven minutes. During that time, Rose shared tearful hugs with his son and with Helms, the Reds' first base coach. Later, after the Reds won and Rose had also tripled and scored twice, Rose said he hadn't intended to cry.

"I was doing all right until I looked up and started thinking about my [late] father," he said. "I saw my father and Ty Cobb looking down on me. I didn't plan on being emotional."

Rose played one more season, retiring as a player at age 45. He finished with 4,256 hits and a .303 batting average. He is also the all-time leader in games played (3,562), plate appearances (15,890), and at-bats (14,053).

Despite his records, Rose is not in the Hall of Fame. Commissioner Bart Giamatti banned Rose from baseball just four years after he passed Cobb. Rose admitted gambling on baseball while serving as Reds manager. Though Rose has tried to get his ban overturned, he remains on the outside looking in.

A GRAND NIGHT

IN THE RICH HISTORY OF MLB NO ONE HAS MATCHED WHAT FERNANDO TATIS DID ON APRIL 23, 1999. IN THE THIRD INNING AT DODGERS STADIUM IN LOS ANGELES, THE ST. LOUIS CARDINALS THIRD BASEMAN TWICE CAME UP WITH THE BASES LOADED. BOTH TIMES HE HOMERED OFF PITCHER CHAN HO PARK. TWO GRAND SLAMS AND EIGHT RUNS BATTED IN (RBIS) IN ONE INNING ARE BOTH RECORDS. FOR TATIS, IT WAS THE HIGHLIGHT OF AN 11-YEAR CAREER. "I CAN'T BELIEVE IT HAPPENED," HE SAID. "I DID NOT EXPECT TO HIT ANOTHER ONE. I'VE NEVER BEEN A HOME RUN HITTER."

5
THE
IRON MAN

In the week leading up to September 6, 1995, Orioles shortstop Cal Ripken Jr. could not sleep. He also had trouble eating. At first he thought he might be sick. Then he decided it was just a case of nerves.

His anxiety was understandable. Ripken was about to break one of baseball's most treasured records, and it seemed as if the whole world was watching. Since May 30, 1982, Ripken had played in every Orioles game. Day games, night games, road games, home games—it did not matter. Even on days when he did not feel his best, Ripken played. And he usually played well. Already he was a two-time AL Most Valuable Player (MVP) and 13-time All-Star.

Cal Ripken Jr., *front*, acknowledges his fans in a ceremony after he played in his 2,131st consecutive game on September 6, 1995.

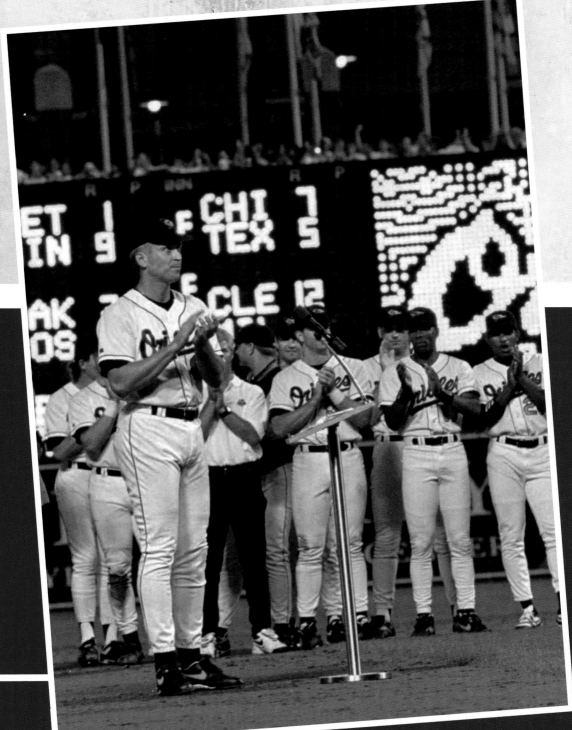

Cal Ripken Jr. hands an autographed ball to President Bill Clinton while Clinton's daughter Chelsea and Vice President Al Gore look on.

As he got out of bed on the morning of September 6, Ripken had played in 2,130 straight games. The night before he had tied Lou Gehrig's record for consecutive games played, set in 1939. Gehrig's streak had long been said to be unbreakable. It was 823 games longer than any other. That adds up to more than five full seasons.

"I don't think anyone will ever break Lou Gehrig's record," said former Dodgers and Padres first baseman Steve Garvey, whose streak of 1,207 games ended in 1983.

"I know I played with a lot of nagging injuries to keep the streak alive, and I didn't even get close."

Ripken had not set out to break a record. He just wanted to play every day. So even when he was hit on the elbow by a pitch in 1992, he stayed in the lineup. He played through a sprained knee in 1993. And as he dealt with assorted ankle and back injuries, he stayed in the lineup every day for more than 14 seasons.

Now he was on the verge of history. Reporters had been following him for weeks. Everyone wanted to hear what Ripken had to say about passing Gehrig, the New York Yankees' legendary "Iron Horse."

There was a festival atmosphere that night at Baltimore's Oriole Park at Camden Yards. Baseball greats Joe DiMaggio, Hank Aaron, Brooks Robinson, and Frank Robinson were on hand. President Bill Clinton and Vice President Al Gore also were there. Red, white, and blue banners decorated the ballpark. Fans filled every one of the 46,272 seats.

Ripken started at shortstop against the California Angels, and the crowd cheered his every move. Fans went crazy when he hit a home run in the fourth inning.

But the real celebration occurred after the final out in the top of the fifth. A baseball game becomes official at that point—it cannot be called off due to bad weather. So at that point, Ripken's streak officially reached 2,131 games.

Dodgers pitcher Orel Hershiser pitches against the San Diego Padres on September 28, 1988, the night he set the record for most consecutive scoreless innings pitched.

A giant banner hanging on the B&O Warehouse beyond the right-field bleachers was changed from "2130" to "2131." Balloons in the Orioles' black and orange colors were released. Ripken stood at the top of the Orioles dugout and waved to the cheering fans. He then walked to the seats behind home plate to hug his family.

A few minutes later, teammates grabbed Ripken and sent him out to greet the fans. Ripken trotted all the way around the warning track, high-fiving and waving. He hugged and shook hands with Angels players and coaches when he reached their dugout.

The game resumed and the Orioles won 4–2. The next day, Ripken, too, resumed playing every day. He continued until he took himself out of the lineup on September 20, 1998. His streak had reached 2,632 games. The 38-year-old Ripken simply said, "It was time."

Three years later he retired with 3,184 hits and 431 homers. In 2007, Ripken was inducted into the Baseball Hall of Fame.

OREL HISTORY

ON AUGUST 30, 1988, DODGERS PITCHER OREL HERSHISER HELD THE MONTREAL EXPOS SCORELESS OVER THE FINAL FOUR INNINGS OF A 4–2 WIN. THE NEXT TIME OUT HE THREW A COMPLETE-GAME SHUTOUT. THEN HE THREW FOUR MORE CONSECUTIVE SHUTOUTS, FOLLOWED BY 10 SCORELESS INNINGS ON THE LAST DAY OF THE SEASON, A 16-INNING LOSS TO SAN DIEGO. HERSHISER THREW 59 CONSECUTIVE SCORELESS INNINGS, BREAKING DON DRYSDALE'S RECORD OF 58 2/3 SCORELESS INNINGS FROM 1968. SOME SAY THE RECORD WILL NOT BE BROKEN, BUT HERSHISER IS NOT ONE OF THEM. "THE CHANCES OF DOING IT ARE 100 PERCENT," HE SAID IN 2013. "BECAUSE I DID IT."

6

THE YANKEE DYNASTY

Deep beyond the right-center field fence at Yankee Stadium in New York is a display like no other in the major leagues. On a gray, brick wall behind the bleachers is a large Yankees logo above a sign that reads "27-Time World Champions." Surrounding the logo are the dates of the World Series titles won by the Yankees.

The first came in 1923. The twenty-seventh was in 2009. In between, the Yankees won like no other team in American pro sports.

Babe Ruth is just one of the many legendary players who helped build

The Yankees' famous monument park honors some of the greatest players in team history.

Babe Ruth first put on the iconic pinstripe uniform in 1920. Ever since then, the Yankees have been powered by baseball's biggest stars. Players such as Lou Gehrig, Joe DiMaggio, Mickey Mantle, Whitey Ford, Reggie Jackson, Mariano Rivera, and Derek Jeter followed, each winning multiple championships.

After their 2009 victory, the Yankees were invited to the White House. During a ceremony, President Barack Obama said that each year the Yankees expect to "win it all."

"Nothing beats that Yankees tradition," the president said. "Twenty-seven World Series titles, 48 Hall of Famers. . . . From Ruth to Gehrig, Mantle to DiMaggio, it's hard to imagine baseball without the long line of legends who've worn the pinstripes."

The team began play in 1903 as the New York Highlanders. They changed their name to the Yankees in 1913, but no matter what they were called, they were not very good. Then in 1921 and 1922 the Yankees won the AL but lost the World Series.

When they won it all in 1923, a new era was launched. The Yankees went on to win multiple World Series championships in every decade but the 1980s. The only other team with more than 10 is the St. Louis Cardinals with 11.

Since the 1920s, the Yankees have had the biggest stars, the grandest ballpark, the highest-paid players, and the most winning teams. The Yankees became a symbol of success. They won the AL pennant 40 times through 2014.

Acquiring Ruth turned the team around. The Yankees purchased him from the Red Sox after the 1919 season. The slugger went on to carry New York to four World Series championships. The 1927 team was perhaps the greatest. Ruth hit a then-record 60 home runs. He was part of the famed "Murderers' Row" lineup that also featured Gehrig, Bob Meusel, and Tony Lazzeri. New York won 110 games, lost only 44, and won the pennant by 19 games.

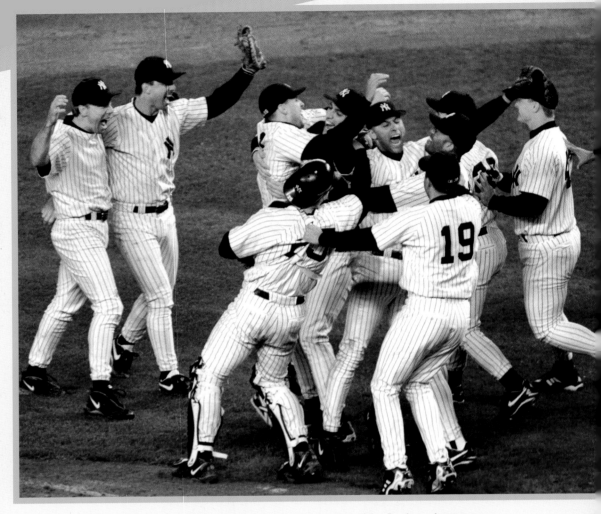

The 1998 Yankees, shown celebrating their AL Championship Series victory over the Cleveland Indians, were one of the greatest teams of all time.

It then swept the Pittsburgh Pirates in the World Series. As baseball historian Leonard Koppett wrote, "No team has ever been any better."

One Yankees team that rivals it came along 71 years later. The 1998 Yankees were 114–48, won their division by 22 games, and went 11–2 in the postseason. They outscored opponents by an average of almost two runs per game. Every starting position player had an on-base percentage of .350 or better. After losing in the playoffs the year before, they were on a mission. "This drove them to the greatest season in the history of baseball," wrote Buster Olney of ESPN. "They crushed teams."

For the Yankees, it was simply their twenty-fourth championship. It was another date on a gray wall dedicated to excellence.

THE GREATEST YANKEE

OF ALL THE YANKEES STARS, BABE RUTH WAS THE BIGGEST. IN HIS FIRST SEASON IN NEW YORK IN 1920, HE HIT 54 HOMERS, ALMOST DOUBLING THE RECORD 29 HE HIT IN 1919. WHEN HE RETIRED IN 1935, RUTH HELD THE RECORD FOR HOMERS IN A SEASON (60) AND A CAREER (714). HE'S STILL FIRST ALL-TIME IN SLUGGING PERCENTAGE (.690). "HE WAS IN A LEAGUE OF HIS OWN," SAID BARRY BONDS, WHO SURPASSED RUTH'S HOME RUN RECORDS. "HE BROUGHT THE GAME AT A DIFFERENT LEVEL."

7
POWERFUL
PUJOLS

St. Louis Cardinals slugger Albert Pujols stared down Texas Rangers relief pitcher Alexi Ogando. The Cardinals led 8–6 in the sixth inning of Game 3 of the 2011 World Series. Pujols wanted to add to that lead.

A chest-high fastball approached. Pujols whipped his bat through the strike zone and connected with full force. The ball rocketed high and deep to left field. It slammed into the second deck 432 feet from home plate.

For just a second, Pujols watched the ball. Then he trotted around the bases. It was a three-run home run. The Cardinals' lead ballooned to 11–6.

Albert Pujols watches his sixth-inning home run soar toward the stands in Game 3 of the 2011 World Series.

Albert Pujols's Game 3 heroics helped the St. Louis Cardinals pull out a tense, seven-game victory over the Texas Rangers in the 2011 World Series.

Pujols, the Cardinals' 31-year-old first baseman, was already a three-time NL MVP with 445 home runs in his 11-year career. He was known as "The Machine" for his consistent excellence. And on that night at Rangers Ballpark in Arlington, Texas, he was just getting started. It would be perhaps the greatest hitting performance in Series history.

In the seventh inning, Pujols hit a two-run homer over the left-center field fence. Then in the ninth he blasted a ball deep into the left-field seats for a solo home run.

Only Babe Ruth and Reggie Jackson had previously hit three home runs in a World Series game. Pujols ended up with five hits, six RBIs, four runs scored, and 14 total bases in the 16–7 victory. His five hits tied a Series record, as did his six RBIs. No one had ever collected as many total bases in a World Series game.

"That's something I'm going to be able to tell my kids and grandkids, that I actually witnessed that in person," Game 3 winning pitcher Lance Lynn said.

MATHEWSON'S MAGIC

THERE HAVE BEEN TREMENDOUS WORLD SERIES PITCHING PERFORMANCES, INCLUDING THE PERFECT GAME THROWN BY THE YANKEES' DON LARSEN IN 1956. BUT FOR EXCELLENCE IN AN ENTIRE SERIES, THE NEW YORK GIANTS' CHRISTY MATHEWSON IS NUMBER ONE. IN 1905 AGAINST THE PHILADELPHIA ATHLETICS, MATHEWSON THREW A RECORD THREE COMPLETE-GAME SHUTOUTS, WINNING 3–0, 9–0, AND 2–0. HE GAVE UP JUST 13 HITS IN 27 INNINGS AND ALLOWED ONLY ONE RUNNER AS FAR AS THIRD BASE.

FUN FACTS

FRUSTRATED CUB

Ernie Banks was a superb and popular player with the Chicago Cubs from 1953 to 1971. He's in the Hall of Fame with 512 home runs. But "Mr. Cub" also holds the record for most games played without ever appearing in a postseason game: 2,528. In fact, Banks's teams finished with a winning record only six times in 19 years.

MR. ERROR

Herman Long, a major league infielder from 1889 to 1904, is known mostly for one thing: he committed the most errors ever, 1,096. In fact, he also had three seasons with 100 or more errors. Yet Long actually was considered a good fielder in his era because he "covered more ground than an automobile," according to one sportswriter of his era. His problems arose once he got to the ball.

SULTAN OF STRIKEOUTS

Over a long career from 1967 to 1987, Reggie Jackson was one of baseball's most feared sluggers. He hit 563 home runs, led his league in homers four times, and was a 14-time All-Star. But he also struck out 2,597 times, the most in MLB history. In fact, Jackson had more strikeouts than hits (2,584).

DUBIOUS HONOR

Jamie Moyer was a good and durable pitcher, winning 269 games from 1986 to 2012. Yet the left-hander gave up 522 home runs, more than any other pitcher in MLB history. One year he gave up 44 in 34 games. Said Moyer: "It's nothing I'm proud of or I'm going to gloat about."

45

GLOSSARY

bleachers
Low-priced seating area for fans beyond the outfield fences.

commissioner
The chief executive of Major League Baseball.

complete game
When a starting pitcher pitches the whole game.

leadoff hitter
The first hitter in a team's lineup.

no-no
Slang term for a no-hitter.

on-base percentage
A measure of a player's ability to get on base through a hit, walk, or being hit by pitch.

shutout
A game in which one team does not score.

slugging percentage
A measure of a player's ability to hit for power.

slump
A long period in which a player does not play up to his usual standards.

switch-hitter
A batter who can hit left-handed or right-handed.

FOR MORE INFORMATION

Goldman, Rob. *Nolan Ryan: The Making of a Pitcher*. Chicago:
 Triumph Books, 2014.

The National Baseball Hall of Fame and Museum. *The Hall: A
 Celebration of Baseball's Greats*. New York: Little Brown and
 Co., 2014.

The New York Times. *The New York Times Story of the Yankees:
 382 Articles, Profiles & Essays from 1903 to the Present*. New
 York: Black Dog & Leventhal Publishers, 2012.

Siwoff, Seymour. *The Elias Book of Baseball Records 2014*. New
 York: Elias Sports Bureau, 2014.

WEBSITES

To learn more about Record Breakers, visit
booklinks.abdopublishing.com. These links are routinely
monitored and updated to provide the most current
information available.

PLACE TO VISIT

National Baseball Hall of Fame and Museum
25 Main Street
Cooperstown, NY 13326
(888) 425-5633
www.baseballhall.org
Officially dedicated on June 12, 1939, the Hall of Fame and
Museum draws about 300,000 people a year to the three-
story facility that includes exhibits about those elected to the
Hall of Fame, as well as memorabilia, photos, and multimedia
presentations about the sport's history, issues, and personalities

INDEX

ABOUT THE AUTHOR

Doug Williams is a freelance writer and former newspaper editor. He lives in San Diego, California, with his wife. He attended his first major league game in 1969, is a lifelong Angels fan, and was lucky enough to be at Game 7 of the 2002 World Series when the Angels won their only championship.